The Collector's Encyclopedia of

OCCUPIED JAPAN
Collectibles

2nd Series

Gene Florence

COLLECTOR BOOKS
A Division of Schroeder Publishing Co., Inc.

The current values in this book should be used only as a guide. They are not intended to set prices, which vary from one section of the country to another. Auction prices as well as dealer prices vary greatly and are affected by condition as well as demand. Neither the Author nor the Publisher assumes responsibility for any losses that might be incurred as a result of consulting this guide.

FOREWORD

"Collecting" things (dolls, beer cans, depression glass, baseball cards, "Occupied Japan" items, hatpins, etc.) has grown to unbelievable proportions in the last decade. Indeed, the fever has gone nation wide. You see the football player on television plugging the collecting of stamps; you pick up a woman's magazine and read an article relating to the collecting of memorabilia of some sort; the local newspapers include a column on identifying collectibles and antiques; several newspapers and magazines have sprung into existence solely to deliver to their readers information about the varying fields of collectibles; and the list goes on and on.

Reasons for this spreading phenomenon are related to people having more time and money to spend; to their having greater mobility than ever before; to there being more flea markets and antique shows placed in their everyday paths at malls, fair grounds, etc.; or to their being caught up in the search for their roots or the nostalgia movement that's swept the country. Too, reports have circulated that there's a fortune in the contents of their attics; or that the value of grandmother's plate collection over the years exceeds the value of her house. For whatever reason, more and more people are "collecting" things of the past; and whether they make money at it or not, most of them will tell you it's fun. There's a thrill or "high" to be reached when you find an intriguing item in your field of collection.

For those of you who may not have the first book, I'm repeating some background information.

All items made in Japan, from the beginning of our occupation at the end of World War II until April 28, 1952, when the occupation ended, that were to be exported to the States had to be marked in one of four ways: "Japan", "Made in Japan", "Occupied Japan" or "Made in Occupied Japan". You can tell that, if all markings were used equally, only half of the items exported during this time period would now be considered collectible. Due to the fact that many Japanese were not overjoyed with the occupation to begin with, it's not too unrealistic to assume that far fewer than half of the items were marked to advertise the fact. In any case, you will find many similar or like items which will offer only "Japan" or "Made in Japan", and thus there is little way of actually proving that the piece was in fact made during the period of time known as the Occupation. When something is made in a limited number or over a limited period of time, someone is bound to be collecting it. This has happened with the items exported with the words "Made in Occupied Japan" stamped on them. The collecting which started quietly at first is now taking voice and being heard throughout the land.

As stated in the first volume, this book is a sampling only of what can be found. You will find many pieces not shown in either book; hopefully, you will be able to find a category which will help you determine a value for what you have.

I would urge you to look for quality pieces when purchasing "Occupied Japan". It has been my experience that finer pieces in any field of collecting hold their value better over the years.

A word of caution was added in the first book and it bears repeating. Be wary of items that have little similarity to what you have been buying. Unscrupulous people have been known to hand stamp "Occupied Japan" onto some pieces. On glazed items, the original mark will be found under the glaze and it will not wash off or remove with nail polish remover. However, on unglazed items, you'll need to exercise some care. Acquaint yourself with styles, coloring, and the types of things available in the field. Study the text and pictures of my two books; they'll give you over 2,300 examples of what to look for in a piece of Occupied Japan. Armed with this information, you should be hard to dupe.

ACKNOWLEDGEMENTS

The story of this book has to belong to my wife, Cathy, who devoted her talents of typing, editing, rewriting and generally turning over the house to **Occupied Japan** for several weeks. To her, readers, you owe this book.

Barbara Benefield of LaGrange, Ga. lent me the stainless steel spoon shown on page 47. The other 1,100 pieces shown in this book belong to me and will soon be found at Grannie Bear Antiques, 120 Clay Avenue in Lexington, Kentucky. Stop in if you are ever in the area.

I would like also to thank James R. Burke, Photography of Lexington for the work he did to get the quality of photographs we have here.

PRICING

All prices shown in this book are retail. These prices were the last thing compiled before this book went to press.

I am aware that you can find higher prices for "Occupied Japan" items than I have in this book; I am also aware that you can still find many pieces at yard sales for considerably less money than a comparable piece here is listed. I have tried to set realistic values for the items I show, prices that reflect the general range I frequently encounter on pieces of "Occupied Japan". I sell "Occupied Japan" items in my shop. I know what price I can sell an item for and what prices will cause the item to sit on the shelf ignored. I've been in several shops over the past few years that have the exact same "Occupied Japan" pieces they had when I first entered their shop years ago. In some cases, I figure they'll still have the pieces in another five years. Their prices are unrealistic in comparison with what is readily available on the market.

Still, this book is meant as a guide only. You, ultimately, will have to decide whether or not a piece you fancy is "worth" the asking price.

Again, prices listed are retail prices; thus, if you want to sell some of your "Occupied Japan" pieces to a dealer, you'll have to discount the items. Most dealers are agreeable to paying you 60% of the latest list price; on certain more desirable pieces, they'll give more, of course.

Prices listed are for mint items, that is, items with no damage. Damaged pieces are useless unless the item is extremely unusual or hard to get.

The cost of living has doubled in the past ten years. The prices of "Occupied Japan" items have doubled in the past five. Does that tell us something?   Happy Hunting!

TABLE OF CONTENTS

PART II FIGURINES

ANIMALS

Collecting animal figurines stamped "Occupied Japan" continues to flourish although finding this particular quarry seems more difficult than in the past. Dogs, birds and frogs appear to head the list as the most desirable types of animals to be found.

Most of the items shown on the following two pages are ceramic. Exceptions are the elephants mounted on wood which are hard plastic and the rubber squeeking Scottie dog pictured on the following page.

Notable on the third row is the cat which is an exact copy of Homer Laughlin's "Harlequin" cat which is selling now for about $25. The cat, itself, is only marked "Japan"; but the bed on which it rests is marked "Occupied Japan". This marking of only one item of a set is a fairly common occurence as most collectors will know.

Of the animals shown in the first book, I was most fond of the baseball playing bears; but my favorites of this second are the mother and baby rabbits pictured on the fourth row. Looking closely you will see that the first rabbit is marked "Niagara"; the second, "Falls"; the third, "Canada"; and the fourth, "1951". This appealed to me for several reasons. It was "Occupied", it was a multiple set, it was a less usually found animal, and it was dated! I could hardly part with my money fast enough!

Top Row:	
Chickens	$ 17.50 - 20.00 pr.
Dog	8.00 - 10.00
Woebegone Horse	9.00 - 11.00
Second Row:	
1st Dog, 7"	12.50 - 15.00
2nd & 3rd Dogs	10.00 - 12.50
Elephant	7.50 - 9.00
Bird	12.00 - 15.00
Third Row:	
Frogs	12.00 - 15.00
Dog	7.00 - 8.00
Cat on Bed/Set	12.00 - 15.00
Lamb	6.00 - 7.00
Fourth Row:	
Frog	10.00 - 12.00
Dog/Set (3)	7.50 - 10.00
Rabbit/Set (4)/Dated	17.50 - 20.00
Fifth Row:	
Bees	6.00 - 7.50
Elephants on Wood/Set	15.00 - 17.50
Cat	4.00 - 5.00
Cat (Black Celluloid)	10.00 - 12.00
Scotties (Celluloid)	6.00 - 8.00

ANIMALS (Con't)

Top Row:

Dogs	12.50 - 15.00
Bird	12.00 - 15.00
Frog (Bisque)	15.00 - 17.50

Second Row:

Birds	7.50 - 9.00
Dog	7.00 - 9.00
Geese (Blue Base, Set 3)	15.00 - 17.50
Goose Pruning Feathers	5.00 - 6.50

Third Row:

Bird	3.00 - 3.50
Dog (Rubber/Scottie)	7.50 - 9.00
Dog and Hydrant	9.00 - 12.50
Penguin	6.00 - 7.00
Dog with Ribbon	7.00 - 8.00

Fourth Row:

Dogs, (First Three)	4.00 - 6.00
Dog (Gray Dachshund, Quality Glaze, Minute Anatomical Detail)	12.00 - 15.00
Dog (Celluloid)	4.00 - 6.00

Fifth Row:

Bird	3.00 - 4.00
Swan	3.00 - 4.00
Monkey	3.50 - 5.00
Deer	5.00 - 6.00
Duck (Humanoid)	12.50 - 15.00

ASH TRAYS - Ceramic

Luck hasn't been with me in finding too many more ceramic ash trays; however, having these around may just invite more people to pollute the air we breathe anyway. So, perhaps a dearth of these is for the best?

The coal scuttle appears again but in a lighter blue color than before. Naturally, the Kentucky souvenir map made me happy; but I expect you'd prefer your state. The "Wedgewood" type this time has the blue and white colors reversed from those commonly seen; and missing from the individual bridge set is the diamond, but I figure that after an interval of thirty years, finding three out of four isn't too bad.

The fish and frog ash trays could possibly be hinting to smokers to drown their habit; the pirate is a cigarette butt snuffer which could double as a small candle holder; and I think the inebriated man with the fly on his nose needs only a cigarette butt on his tongue to make him totally obnoxious.

Top Row:
Cigarette Box and Tray	$ 17.50 - 20.00
Coal Scuttle and Tray	15.00 - 17.50

Second Row:
Pirate Snuffer	7.50 - 9.00
Man with Fly on Nose	15.00 - 17.50
Kentucky Map	12.00 - 15.00

Third Row:
Frog on Lily Pad	10.00 - 12.50
Elephants with Trays	17.50 - 20.00
"Wedgewood-Like" Tray	10.00 - 12.50
Fish	3.00 - 5.00
Bridge Set	3.00 - 3.50 ea.

ASH TRAYS (Metal) and METALLIC OBJECTS

Metallic objects of all sizes and descriptions have been turning up in a range from those shown here to big objects such as bicycles and sewing machines.

Most of the items pictured on the next couple of pages are self explanatory. The range of quality in these items goes from very poor to a fairly high workmanship.

Notice the piano on the next page which serves as a cigarette dispenser once your turn the side handle.

Top Row:

Sugar and Creamer on a Tray	$ 15.00 - 20.00
Cowboy Hat Ash Tray (5″ Width)	8.00 - 10.00
Candlestick, Pair	15.00 - 17.50
Tumbler (5 Oz.)	6.00 - 7.50

Second Row:

Desk Set (Exceptional Quality)	25.00 - 30.00
Match or Cigarette Holders	5.00 - 6.00

Third Row:

Piano Jewelry Holder	15.00 - 17.50
Candy Container (Handled)	12.00 - 15.00
Antimony Desk Set	25.00 - 30.00

Fourth Row:

Ash Tray	3.00 - 3.50
Ash Tray, Souvenir of Alaska	5.00 - 6.00

ASH TRAYS (Metal) and METALLIC OBJECTS

(Con't.)

Top Row:

Dragon Mug (Engraved "Sue")	$ 12.00 - 15.00
Cigarette Holder	4.00 - 5.00
Tea or Spice Canister	10.00 - 12.00

Second Row:

Leaf Candy Dish	10.00 - 12.00
Salt & Pepper Shakers	8.00 - 10.00
Salt & Pepper Shakers on Tray	10.00 - 12.00
Open Candy Dish	8.00 - 10.00
Piano Cigarette Dispenser	20.00 - 25.00

Third Row:

Jewelry Boxes, 5 Assorted Sizes	10.00 - 15.00
Open Candy Dish	10.00 - 12.00
Hand Warmer & Chamois Bag	25.00 - 30.00
Butter Dish	12.50 - 15.00
Sugar & Creamer, Pair	12.50 - 15.00

Fourth Row:

Cowboy Ash Tray	3.50 - 5.00
Heart Ash Tray (Hot Springs, Ark.)	4.00 - 5.00
Cowboy Hat Ash Tray (3" Wide)	5.00 - 6.00

CELLULOID and DOLLS

Items shown in this category cross the boundaries of several fields of collecting. Doll and toy collectors, for instance, would be interested in several of the items regardless of the fact that they are "Occupied Japan". Since toy items are doubly collectible, the demand for them is increased; and thus, the prices have risen accordingly. Celluloid items fit this doubly desired category also as there are collectors who look just for celluloid objects.

On the following page, the stagecoaches and rickshaw are hard plastic; and, of course, those Christmas bulbs are not celluloid, a highly flammable substance.

Santa and his reindeer came in the original box; the bell rings.

The small (two inch) football figure is a pin to be worn at football games with an appropriate colored ribbon of the home team.

The water lily came from a warehouse in Hawaii. It seems that Japanese items understandably didn't sell well there back then and the owner just packed up those items and stashed them away in a warehouse where they recently constituted quite a "find". The lilies, in various colors, float in a bowl of water and were to be used as party centerpieces.

The Halloween goggles were found while on vacation in South Carolina which just proves collectors never vacation from collecting.

Top Row:
Red Haired Doll	$ 30.00 - 35.00
Blue Dressed Doll	25.00 - 30.00
Japanese Set of Dolls in Box	50.00 - 55.00

Second Row:
Football Player Doll	12.00 - 15.00
Baseball Players	12.00 - 15.00
Doll in White Gown	35.00 - 40.00

Third Row:
Pink Teddy Bear	17.50 - 20.00
Doll in Blue (3″ Composition)	25.00 - 30.00
Cat, Dog, Camel	9.00 - 10.00 ea.

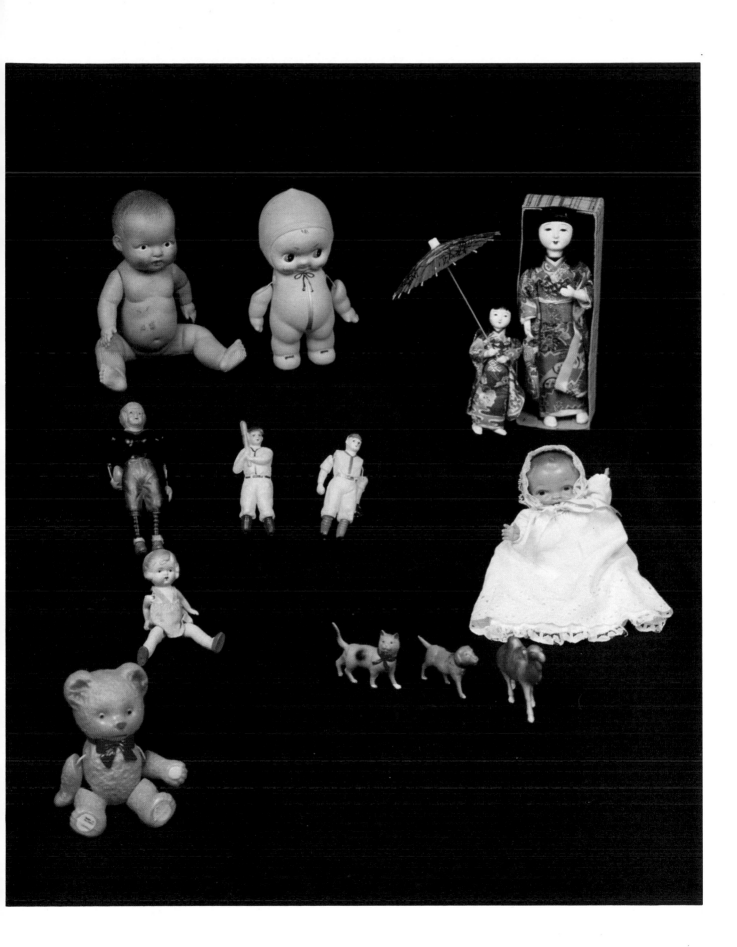

CELLULOID and DOLLS (Con't.)

Top Row:

Mechanical Santa and Reindeer	$ 35.00 - 40.00
Football Pin	6.00 - 7.00
Rudolph, 7″	15.00 - 17.50
Small Reindeer	7.50 - 8.50

Second Row:

Rickshaw	12.00 - 15.00
Mechanical Santa	30.00 - 35.00

Third Row:

Stagecoaches	12.00 - 15.00
Goggles	6.00 - 7.50
Floating Water Lily	5.00 - 7.00
Mechanical Scottie with Shoe	20.00 - 22.50
Christmas Bulbs in Box	17.50 - 20.00

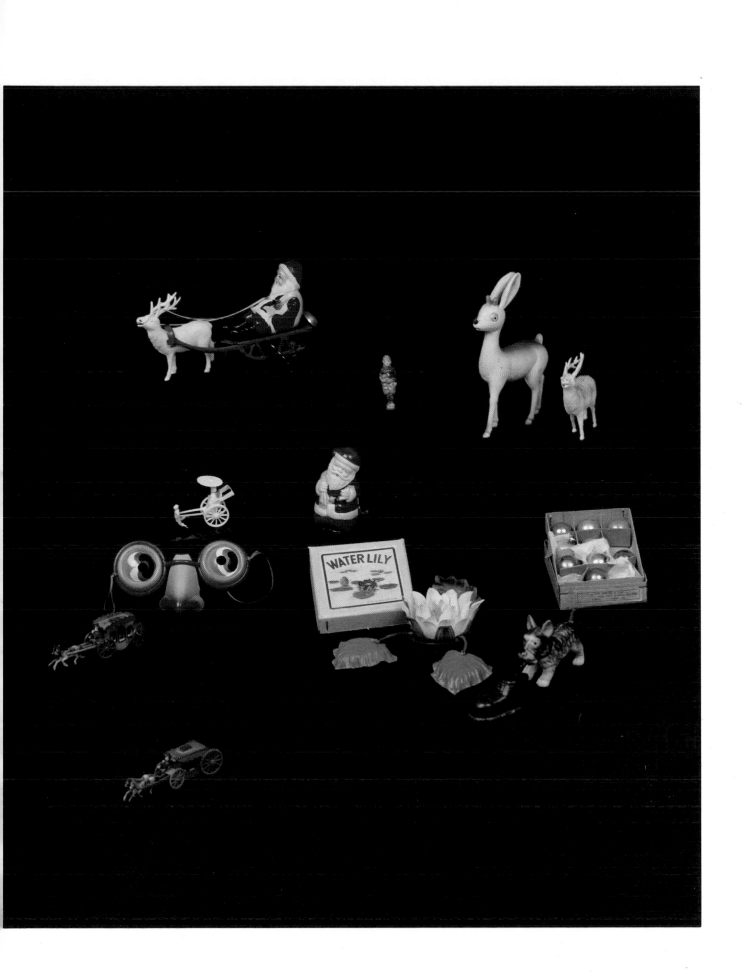

CHILDREN'S TEA SETS and DOLL ITEMS

Children's dishes, ever an item of nostalgic value, have gained even more importance in the wave of doll and toy collecting sweeping the country. The miniature tea sets to be found with "Occupied Japan" markings, for instance, are coveted by many doll collectors as items for their doll houses; too, these particular items are often grabbed by miniature collectors as well. Again, we "Occupied" collectors face competition from other sources as happens in many of the categories.

Most of the miniature tea sets come with trays on which a teapot, creamer and sugar reside. These sets vary from rather clever detail to extremely crude, lopsided versions. The pottery-like green set shown here fits this latter category, but the material intrigued me as I had not previously encountered one made of this substance.

The prized Donald Duck set is a four place setting in the original box! Boxes are important, collectors! One feels doubly blessed when the original box is there even if it shows somewhat shabby treatment; so, don't pitch out the original boxes as one lady told me she had done! Again, there are collectors outside the area of "Occupied Japan" who would dearly love to possess this set because of the cartoon character depicted. (I've heard of a Mickey Mouse set like this one; but I've been unable to trace it to its source. Perhaps you'll have better luck than I!)

Tea Sets
  Place Settings*

Two	$ 17.50 - 20.00
Three	25.00 - 30.00
Four	35.00 - 40.00
Four with Toureen and Platter	45.00 - 50.00
Five	55.00 - 60.00
Six	65.00 - 75.00

* Especially colorful sets or sets such as the Donald Duck will bring twenty to twenty-five percent more per setting.

Tray, Sugar, Creamer, Teapot	$ 22.00 - 25.00
Tray, Sugar and Creamer	17.50 - 20.00
Bath Set, 3 Pieces	20.00 - 22.50

CUP and SAUCER SETS

Prices for the more colorful cup and saucer sets have risen drastically at the antique shows and flea markets I have attended lately. Demitasse cups and saucers, in particular, seem to have attracted more devotees from the rank and file collectors of "Occupied Japan".

Remember, due to the Japanese penchant for making things attractive to the eye of the beholder, the interior of these cups is often as attractive as the exterior. They were made thus to please you as you drank from them. One collector fumed that she had a fortune tied up in wire cup and saucer racks, but it was the only way she could devise of properly showing the interiors of the cups!

The fourth cup on the second row is decorated with a Satsuma-like pattern while the last cup in the third row is of the famed Blue Willow pattern. These two are probably the most widely known of all the Japanese patterns.

Top Row:

1st and 5th Sets, Hexagonal	$ 10.00 - 12.50
2nd Set	6.00 - 7.50
3rd and 4th Sets	7.00 - 8.50

Second Row:

1st Cup Only	8.00 - 9.00
2nd Set	10.00 - 12.50
3rd Set	12.50 - 15.00
4th (Satsuma) Set	17.50 - 20.00
5th Dragon Set	15.00 - 17.50

Third Row:

1st, 3rd, 4th Sets	10.00 - 12.50
2nd Set, Flower Petal	17.50 - 20.00
5th Set, Blue Willow	12.00 - 15.00

Fourth Row:

1st, 4th, 5th Sets	10.00 - 12.50
2nd, 3rd Sets	12.50 - 15.00

DECORATIVE ITEMS

Items pictured range in quality from mediocre to that of fine German made china. The painting of the pastoral scene showing the three ladies (on the plate in the center) is particularly fine workmanship. Also, the five part, stacking sweetmeat set would pass for much earlier and finer antique glassware than a mere thirty year old "Occupied Japan" piece!

I have received several reports of electric clocks bearing the "Occupied Japan" marking since the showing of the cuckoo clock in the first book. However, this is the only one I have run across. The clock is made by Sessions, but the china clock case is marked "Occupied".

Top Row:

Sweetmeat	$ 90.00 -100.00
Clock	45.00 - 50.00

Second Row:

Pastoral Scene Plate	65.00 - 75.00
Fall and Spring Plates	12.50 - 15.00 ea.
Square Plate	10.00 - 12.50

DECORATIVE ITEMS (Con't.)

Top Row:
Gold Decorated Plate $ 15.00 - 17.50
Pagoda Plate   12.00 - 13.50

Second Row:
Scenic Plate   8.00 - 10.00
Octagonal Plate   10.00 - 12.50
Small Leaf Plate   3.50 - 4.50

Third Row:
Square Bowl   12.50 - 15.00
Plate with Ladies   17.50 - 20.00
Maple Leaf Plate   5.50 - 7.50
Japanese Scenic Plate   15.00 - 17.50
Flowered Bowl   8.00 - 10.00

Fourth Row:
Small Star Shaped Items   4.00 - 5.50

DINNERWARE SETS

One of the few complaints I got about the first volume was that only one dinnerware set was shown. I've tried to remedy that situation this time. Five of the sets shown are complete although they aren't shown as such. Instead we chose to give you a sampling of what was available so the photographer could get close enough to also give you an idea of the pattern.

The sets shown range from four place settings to twelve. Where possible, we've included the serving pieces. You will notice style and shape differences; but there are similarities between the patterns also. Notice the covered tureens and the gravy boats with their attached trays. Most of the sets are good quality china; however, the "Iris" set is a heavy stoneware.

Complete sets are hard to find. For instance, the "Wild Rose" set by Fuji China shown on the next page is missing several cups, etc. I particularly mention this here because my wife claimed it when I first brought it home; but in two years, we've not been able to find another piece; and with only six settings, it's not practical to use at this point. So, if you've some for sale, please get in touch!.

The sets are shown as follows:
"Wild Rose" by Fuji China, Page 29
"Forget-Me-Not" by Aladdin Fine China, Page 30
"Iris" and "Bamboo", Hand Crafted, Page 31
"Orange Blossom" by Kent China, Page 32
"Rochelle" by Grace China, Page 33

I'm giving "ball park" figures for these sets according to what I paid and according to china beauty and overall pieces to the set.

4 Place Setting with Serving Pieces	$125.00 - 150.00
6 Place Setting with Serving Pieces	200.00 - 250.00
8 Place Setting with Serving Pieces	250.00 - 300.00
12 Place Setting with Serving Pieces	300.00 - 500.00

I personally consider the stoneware to be less valuable than the china; a stoneware lover may not care for that statement; but I find more customers buy the china sets than the stoneware ones.

DINNERWARE (Con't.)

This all may look like "Blue Willow" to you; however, each of these pieces have different markings from "Willoware" to "Blue Willow"; so it may be difficult to match pieces if you're a purist. There is also a demitasse cup in this pattern shown under the cup and saucer sets. The cup and saucer pictured here is a copy of an English pattern called "Old Willoware"; I'm assuming there is a setting of this pattern available also.

The floral bowl is marked "Gold Castle" which I frankly don't know whether it is the company name or the pattern name. However, since it's a soup bowl, I presume there is more of this to be had somewhere.

Notice the creamer and sugar sets pictured elsewhere in the book. They may well belong to a particular set of china.

Not pictured, but commonly found, is a pattern which features little rust diamond shapes all around the edges and I believe it's called "Fine Diamond". I've run into it more than any one pattern in "Occupied Japan" dinnerware.

"Blue Willow" Grill Plate	$ 10.00 - 12.00
Salad Plate	6.00 - 8.00
Platter	20.00 - 25.00
"Old Willoware" Cup and Saucer	12.00 - 15.00
"Gold Castle" Soup Bowl	6.00 - 8.00

FISH BOWL ITEMS

Shown in the glass jar at the top is what is known as a time period item. You place these shriveled up looking little spots of color into water and gradually, over a period of "time", they "bloom". They would be pretty in a fish tank, but I frankly don't know if the dyes used are fish safe or not. (No, the jar is not "Occupied Japan"; neither is the glass bowl used as prop for the celluloid lily.)

Speaking of the lily pond, you will notice an acrobatic young man and a frog are both "hanging about" so to speak. I doubt the young man is as interested in gaining the lily pond as he is in gaining a vantage point from which to view the sunning mermaid!

Top Row:
Blooming Flower $ 3.00 - 5.00

Second Row:
Frog Hanger   15.00 - 20.00
Man Hanger   12.50 - 15.00
Mermaid   15.00 - 17.50
Floating Water Lily   5.00 - 7.00

Third Row:
Ship   7.50 - 9.00
Arches   10.00 - 12.50

GLASS OBJECTS

In the three years since the first book, I have only been able to find these glass objects; and six small animals and five of the perfume bottles were bought in groups at one time. Therefore, I conclude, as before, that glass "Occupied Japan" items are as scarce as the proverbial hen's teeth.

Each of the small glass animals has a small sticker on them else they would be impossible to distinguish from later made animals.

The glass wind chimes came in a marked box and one of the chimes has a painted on "Made in Occupied Japan" decoration.

The girl in the center holds a glass egg timer; hence her inclusion.

Top Row:
Wind Chimes $ 25.00 - 30.00

Second Row:
Pink Cologne   17.50 - 20.00
Small Animals with Sticker   7.00 - 7.50
Perfume Bottles   17.50 - 20.00

Third Row:
Perfume Bottles   17.50 - 20.00
Salt & Pepper Shakers   12.50 - 15.00
Girl with Egg Timer   12.50 - 15.00

Fourth Row:
Toy Binoculars   15.00 - 17.50
Perfume & Atomizer Set   35.00 - 40.00
Perfume Bottle   17.50 - 20.00
Mustard & Lid   15.00 - 17.50

LACQUERWARE

Expensively priced in the early 1950's, this ware did not sell well and there are several hoards of it that have been found stored in warehouses in Hawaii and even one in Connecticut.

A sample cup to show the layers of wood has been placed in the center of the photograph.

Cups, saucers, wine goblets and trays in gold, red and black have been turning up more and more at "class" antique shows in dealer's booths who would "die dead off" before displaying most "Occupied Japan" items. They usually have "class" prices on the items as well. I saw a lovely pair of Chinese red lacquerware bud vases at one show, about seven inches tall, for a mere $65.00. They are conspicuous only by their absence from this photograph; or perhaps, after buying the five part tray, I was just too stubborn to spend that much for one picture. I admit to gleefully noting that said vases hadn't sold by show's end, however!

This type ware is some of the finest workmanship to come out of Japan during this era. You tend to find two veins of thought about it still. One either loves it dearly or hates it with a passion. There seems to be little middle ground.

Top Row:
Tray, Five Part, Handled/Very Heavy	$ 65.00 - 75.00
Wine Goblet	12.00 - 15.00

Second Row:
Cup and Saucer, Sets	15.00 - 17.50
Bowl and Spoon (Missing Underplate)	12.50 - 15.00

LAMPS - Bisque

Occupied Japan lamps are usually found in matched pairs. When a male and female figure occur, the man, in true gentlemanly fashion, stands to the outside of each so that the figures are mirror images of each other.

The lamps at the top in bisque are exceedingly fine. The same couple appears on the next page in porcelain. The porcelain are a trifle more colorful and photographed well. However, close up, I prefer the bisque.

The "Wedgewood" imitation lamps are the first I've seen. One is adorned with flower-like decals. You will recall that this look was very popular in the early fifties.

Anyone having the mate to the adorable "Mary Had A Little Lamb" lamp, please get in touch. I've been told it is "Little Boy Blue", but I rather suspect it may be Mary and the lamb reversed. However, I know that children's lamps were more often than not sold as singles; so pairing may be an impossible dream. In any case, I'd be interested in finding out.

The gold lamp base on the following page, partially hidden, is unusual in that it is a fish which appears to float on its fins.

Shades for these lamps have been removed to show the detail.

Top Row:
Bisque Lamps, Paired	$ 45.00 - 50.00 ea.; 125.00 pr.
2nd Lamp	32.50 - 37.50

Second Row:
Mary and Lamb	45.00 - 50.00
"Wedgewood" Types	52.50 - 55.00 ea.

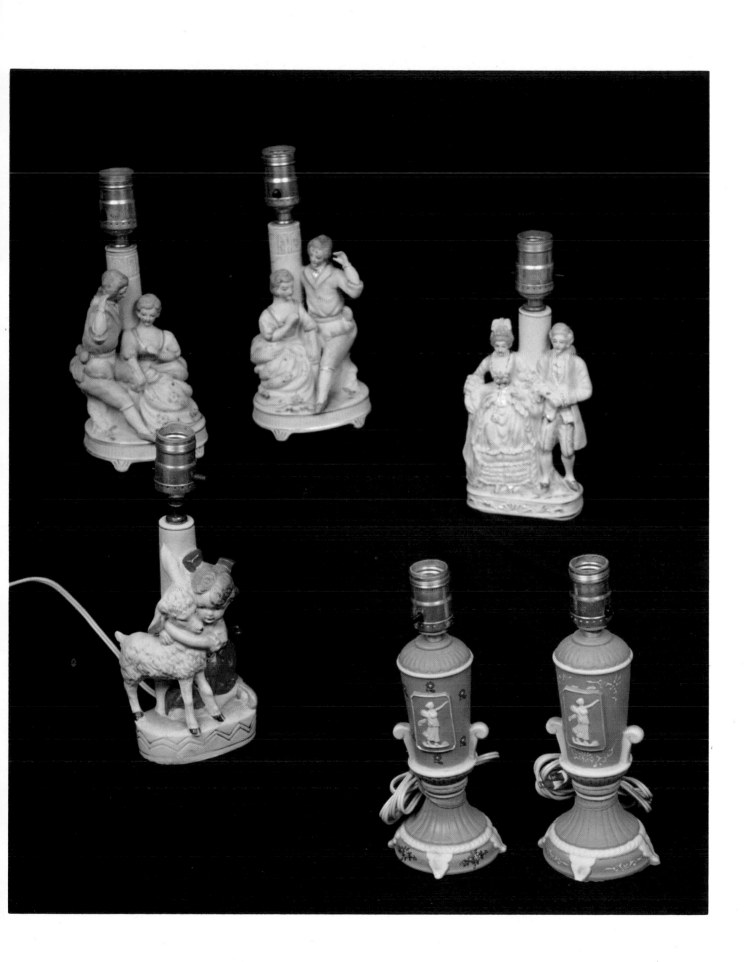

LAMPS - Porcelain

Top Row:

Standing Colonial Couple	$ 32.50 - 37.50 ea.; 85.00 pr.
Seated Colonial Couple	35.00 - 40.00 ea.; 90.00 pr.

Second Row:

Oriental Dancer	22.50 - 25.00
Colonial Lady	17.50 - 22.50
Colonial Couple	20.00 - 25.00
Lamp Base with Fish Inset	22.50 - 25.00

LIGHTERS and MISC. METALLIC OBJECTS

Since the last book, I have found more unusual and entertaining objects in this one category than in any other. I never expected to find a skillet marked "Occupied Japan" or a belt buckle that doubles as a cigarette lighter. The latter seems to bring to fore a whole gamut of possibilities if you were wearing such a buckled belt and your lady friend needed a light. It would take some practice to use however, as one might conceivably light the wrong butt.

The telephones "dial" to open and close the lighter.

The top of the bottle flips its lid to reveal a lighter in the champagne bucket and bottle combination.

The bullet shaped container is a carrier for four "shot" glasses.

The stainless steel spoon was borrowed from a collector in Georgia, who, by the way, would like to have more of them. It's marked on the back "Desco Stainless Occupied Japan".

Top Row:
Telephone Cigarette Lighter	$ 17.50 - 20.00
Cast Metal Skillet and Handle	15.00 - 17.50

Second Row:
Champagne Bottle Lighter	17.50 - 20.00
Football Lighter	12.50 - 15.00
Belt Buckle Lighter	30.00 - 35.00

Third Row:
Letter Opener and Case	12.50 - 15.00
Miniature Lighter	8.50 - 10.00
Miniature Harmonica on Chain	8.00 - 10.00
Hav-A-Shot, Bullet Carrier & Glasses	15.00 - 20.00
Buddha Gods	5.00 - 7.50 ea.
Spoon, Desco Stainless	1.50 - 2.50
Horse and Rider	15.00 - 17.50

Bottom Row:
Pliers in Original Box	18.00 - 20.00
Wrench in Original Box	18.00 - 20.00

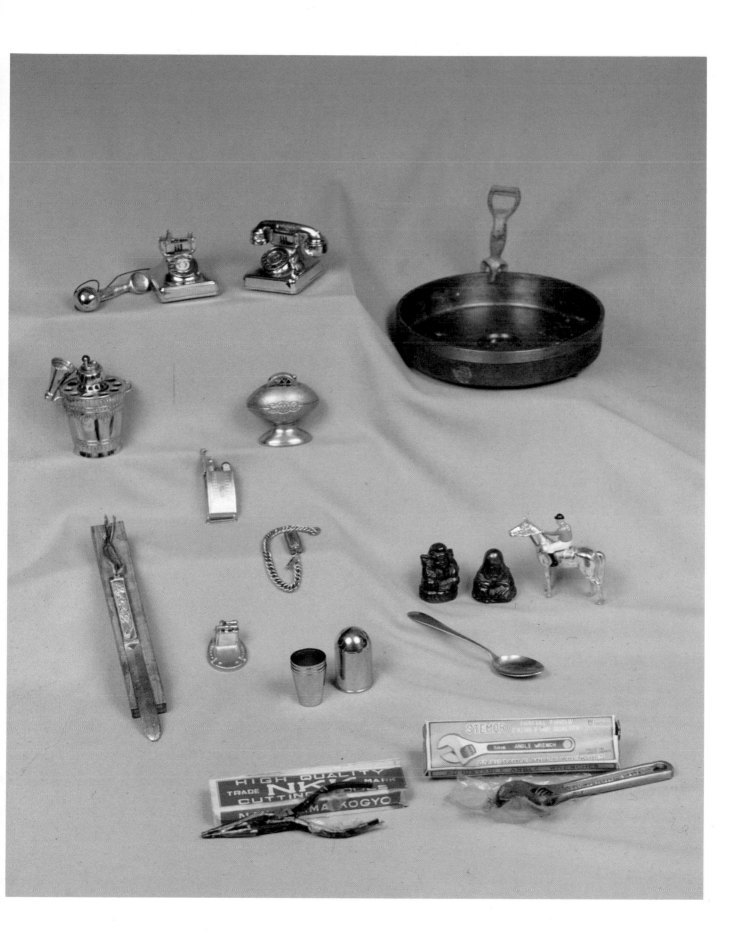

NOVELTY ITEMS

Cheap, souvenir items are the most abundantly found "Occupied Japan" glassware though figurines run a close second. The souvenir pieces are responsible mostly for the "Junkey" image that most people carry in their minds when mention is made of being a collector of "Occupied Japan". It was "junk" and in some sense, still is; and, yet, because of its age, marking and whimsical appeal, its value is many times the $.19 price markings that many of the items still carry.

For instance, the black people items are fast disappearing and are highly sought after no matter their crudity of design. Shoe collectors prize the variety of little, ornate shoes. Souvenir pieces bearing the name of one's own particular locale are delighted finds of collectors. I particularly enjoyed finding the little pitcher with the horse saying 'Kentucky'; no doubt someone from Cody, Wyoming, would better appreciate the other pitcher. Thus, for various reasons, the cheap, junkey, if you will, souvenir pieces are very collectible.

Notice the egg cups and the heart shaped box. I thought they were a little out of the ordinary.

Top Row:

Negro Outhouse	$ 18.00 - 20.00
Blue Pitchers	2.50 - 4.00
Clocks	3.00 - 5.00
Grandfather Clock	9.00 - 11.00

Second Row:

Blue Teakettle (Lid Lifts)	3.50 - 5.00
Souvenir Pitchers	3.00 - 4.00
Other Items	2.00 - 4.00

Third Row:

Shoes (Note the cat heads on two.)	5.00 - 6.50

Fourth Row:

1st, 4th, 5th Shoes	3.50 - 4.50
2nd Bisque Shoe	10.00 - 12.00
3rd Shoe, Out Door Scene	8.00 - 9.50

Fifth Row:

Egg Cups	12.00 - 15.00
Piano (2 Part)	6.00 - 8.00
Dutch Clog Shoe Planter	5.00 - 6.00
Bench	2.50 - 3.00

Sixth Row:

Stroller, Soldiers, Shoe	4.00 - 5.00
Covered Wagon	5.00 - 7.00
Heart Box (2 Piece)	10.00 - 12.00
Cinderella Coach and Horses	12.50 - 15.00

PAPER, WOOD, et. al.

Colorful fans which could well be "Occupied Japan" abound. No one ever seemed to toss them out. However, on many the mark is nearly faded off as the ink used didn't stand the passage of time. Too, I've found a few that had a paper sticker applied; naturally, most of those have long since gone.

The Army and Navy needles shown here were seemingly never used.

On the paper in the center are individual shamrocks made of wire and thin string which were intended to be sold in the dime stores at 2 for $.05 — to keep one from getting pinched for not wearing green on St. Patrick's Day! They each bear a tiny white sticker saying "Made in Occupied Japan". These and the prayer beads next to them were given me compliments of a reader in California who thought they'd be interesting to collectors.

The white, squarish item above the red prayer beads is a whetstone for sharpening knives and scissors to whittle wood and to cut paper?

Needle and thread are found within the confines of the smaller pincushion.

Top Row:	
Fans	$ 8.00 - 10.00
Coolie Pincushion	17.50 - 20.00
Second Row:	
Whetstone	8.00 - 10.00
Boat	12.00 - 15.00
Shamrocks	1.00 - 1.50 ea.
Prayer Beads	15.00 - 20.00
Sewing Kit	12.00 - 15.00
Bottom Row:	
Needle Packets	8.00 - 10.00

The Army and Navy

Needle Book
Contains a full variety of
Large Eyed Needles

The Holiday

Needle Assortment

PAPER and WOOD (Con't.)

Top Row:
Picnic Basket $ 55.00 - 65.00

Second Row:
Cigarette Dispenser   20.00 - 25.00
Trays   4.00 - 5.00 ea.

Third Row:
Bamboo Dipper   17.50 - 20.00
Salad Bowl   6.00 - 7.50
Coaster Box and 6 Coasters   12.00 - 15.00

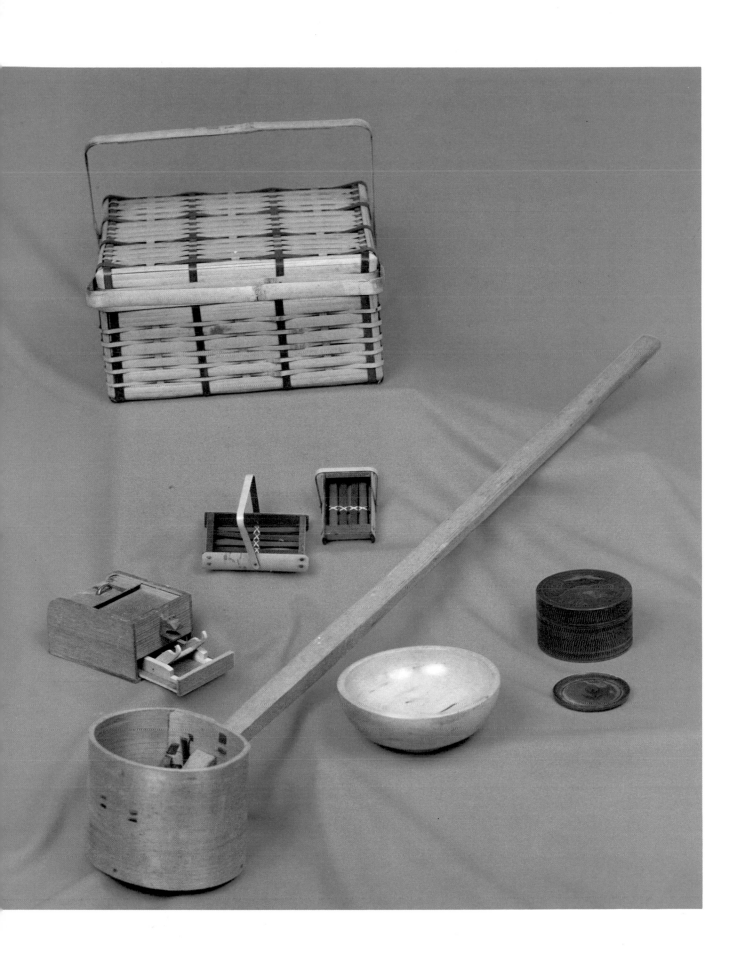

PAPER MACHE and PURSES

These trays, marked "Alcohol Proof" on the back, are readily found — but usually not in such pristine shape as these.

In a collection of over five hundred pieces I found the Jack-O-Lantern. This mustachioed version rather appealed to me.

Most of the beaded purses found are in a sad state of repair. Should you find one, ladies, nice enough to still use, you should examine it often to make certain the beading is intact. Nylon thread was not in use then and cotton thread weakens with age; so extra special care would be required in using one now.

Top Row:
Tray	$ 4.00 - 5.50
Jack-O-Lantern	30.00 - 35.00

Second Row:
Coaster	1.50 - 2.00
Purses	20.00 - 25.00

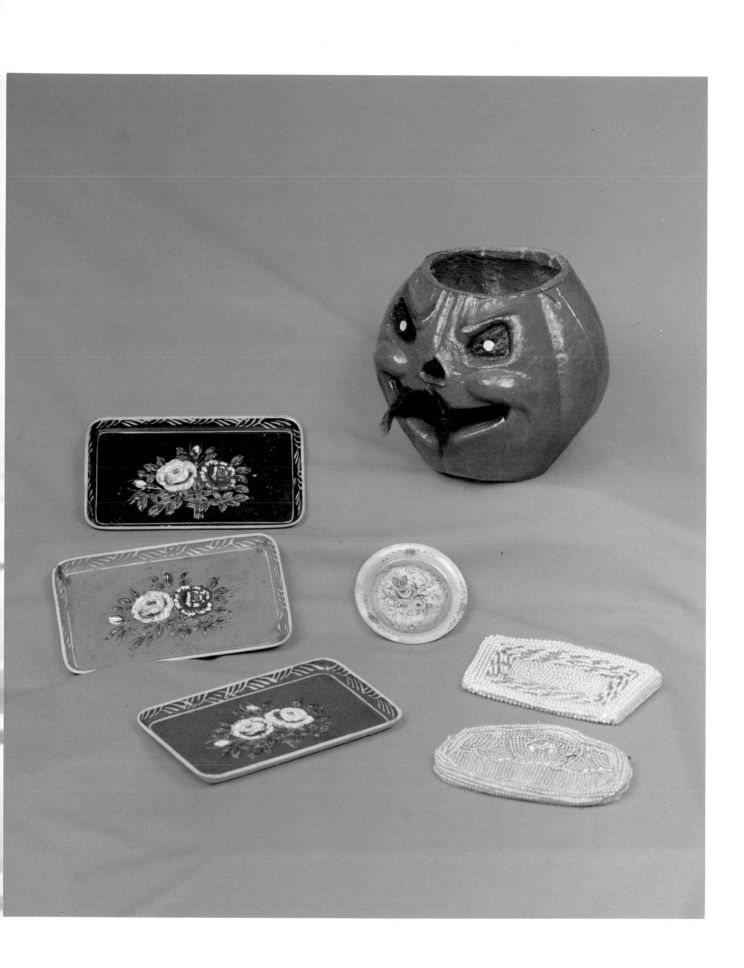

PLANTERS

Planter supplies are fast dwindling whether due to the plant mania enveloping many homes or to more people buying up the cheaper pieces of "Occupied Japan" I don't know.

Several of these planters are a cut above the usual porous, easily chipped type commonly found. In this latter category notice particularly the Lion on the first shelf and the turbaned Sudanese heads.

Top Row:

Dog and Hat	$ 4.50 - 5.00
Elephant and Lion	8.00 - 10.00 ea.
Dutch and Mexican Boy	8.00 - 10.00

Second Row:

Sassy Girl (Boy Companion Pictured Elsewhere)	12.50 - 15.00
Black Girl	30.00 - 35.00
Pig and Rabbit	8.00 - 10.00 ea.
Dog	4.00 - 5.00
Cat	4.00 - 5.00

Third Row:

Donkey Pulling Cart	8.00 - 10.00
Girl and Fat Boy	10.00 - 12.50
Train	7.00 - 8.00
Dog	4.00 - 5.00

Fourth Row:

Sudanese Heads	17.50 - 20.00 ea.
Prim Lady and Tearful Girl	10.00 - 12.00
Man with Wheelbarrow	6.00 - 7.00
Duck	7.00 - 8.00

PLAQUES

Wall plaques were commonly made as pairs; finding them that way and in mint condition is increasingly more difficult. Don't pass a particularly fine plaque by just because its mate isn't available. It is possible to match them up later; and its a thrill like no other in collecting to find a missing mate! Often the pairs are of opposite sexes; so to mate them properly, one must take into consideration overall shapes, colors, attitude of pose, base designs, etc.

You can find plaques in various kinds of material from cheap, easily chipped plaster to very fine bisque. Oddly enough, the cheaper chalkware plaques in mint condition are likely to be as dear as the bisque due to most of these having long since incurred damage.

Top Row:
Japanese Pair, Chalkware	$ 15.00 - 20.00 ea.; 45.00 pr.
Oriental Bisque, Relief	20.00 - 25.00 ea.; 55.00 pr.

Second Row:
Iris Wall Pocket	12.50 - 15.00
Dutch Pair, Chalkware	15.00 - 20.00 ea.; 45.00 pr.
Cupped Saucer	5.00 - 7.50

PLAQUES

Top Row:
Rectangular, Relief Pastoral
 Scene, Bisque (Probably one of
 a pair.) $ 30.00 - 35.00

Second Row:
Round, Relief Musical
 Couple, Bisque   20.00 - 25.00 ea.; 60.00 pr.
Swingers, Relief   17.50 - 20.00 ea.; 45.00 pr.

Third Row:
Heads, Crinoline Lined   17.50 - 20.00 ea.; 45.00 pr.
Standing Colonials, Relief   17.50 - 20.00 ea.; 45.00 pr.

Fourth Row:
Fall and Spring Plaques   6.00 - 8.00 ea.

SALT and PEPPER SHAKERS

Since collecting cute salt and pepper shakers was a common practice long before other types of collecting became fashionable, most "Occupied Japan" salt and pepper shakers have been swallowed up already; and three and four part sets including the little mustard jars have all but vanished. Please remember that usually only the plate or carrying piece of the three and four part sets is marked. The other items tend to say "Japan" only.

I have found several boxed pairs of shakers this time where only the box carries the "Made in Occupied Japan" label. The shakers themselves bear only the "Japan" marking. In cases such as these, saving the box is imperative; otherwise, all you have is a pair of Japanese made salt shakers of which there must be forty trillion.

Top Row:

Fruit Shakers (3 Part)	$ 10.00 - 12.50
Fireside Shakers (5 Part, Include Mustard)	20.00 - 25.00
Flowers (3 Part)	15.00 - 20.00

Second Row:

Cats and Birds, Per Pair	10.00 - 12.00
Dutch Children	12.00 - 15.00

Third Row:

1st, 2nd Pair, Per Pair	8.50 - 10.00
Strawberry Set (3 Part)	12.50 - 15.00
Toby Mug Type, Pair	17.50 - 20.00

Fourth Row:

All Pairs, Per Pair	10.00 - 12.50

Fifth Row:

All Pairs, Per Pair	9.00 - 10.00

SUGAR, CREAMER and TEAPOTS

An abundance of individual teapots have surfaced particularly in the brown glaze.

I'm particularly fond of the English inspired toby in the top row; however, I'd like him a lot better if he still had his lid.

Top Row:
Creamer	$ 9.00 - 11.00
Toby Teapot	35.00 - 45.00

Second Row:
Floral Creamers	12.00 - 14.00
Sugar, Creamer on Tray	25.00 - 27.50

Third Row:
Sugar and Creamer Sets	25.00 - 27.50

Fourth Row:
Tea Pots	10.00 - 12.50
Sugar and Creamer Set	17.50 - 22.50

TEA SETS et. al.

Tea sets include teapot, creamer, sugar and either four or six cups, saucers and plates; and most of them are impossible to find complete. The one pictured here came with a sugar bowl which didn't match suggesting a "marriage" at some previous date.

As far as I know, this picture shows the cottage set complete. It includes the tray for the mustard and the butter dish which were not shown in the first book.

The cased salt, pepper and mustard with spoon gift set appears older than its "Occupied Japan" mark due to the cobalt colored glass.

Top Row:
Tea Set with 4 Cups, Saucers, Plates $100.00 - 125.00
         with 6 Cups, Saucers, Plates   125.00 - 150.00
Gift Set in Case (Cobalt Blue Glass)   30.00 - 40.00

Second Row:
Cottage Set (As Shown)   120.00 - 150.00

TOBIES and OTHER MUGS

The imagination of the Japanese as shown just in the field of "Occupied Japan" period merchandise is a source of constant amazement. Viewing just these Toby mugs we go from devil to parson and from pretty ladies to dogs; and if that isn't enough range of creativity to ponder, take a look at the striptease show presented on the six white mugs. Now, to really boggle the mind, I'll tell you I bought five at one time in Ohio and found the correct missing link mug at a flea market in Tennessee!

The mugs with human or animal form handles are clever and very marketable. You will notice that the brown glazed mug with the flower motif and nude lady handle has a certain grace or beauty of line; it is "eye pleasing", ever a theme of these people.

Top Row:	
Set of Six Mugs	$ 90.00 -100.00
Third Row:	
Dog Tobies	15.00 - 17.50
Lady	10.00 - 12.00
Skull	12.50 - 15.00
Devil	25.00 - 30.00
Fourth Row:	
1st Toby	15.00 - 17.50
2nd Toby	17.50 - 20.00
Indian	25.00 - 30.00

TOBIES and OTHER MUGS (Con't.)

Top Row:

Stein Imitation	$ 13.00 - 15.00
Bunny Handled Mug	17.50 - 20.00
Endowed Lady Handled Mug	20.00 - 25.00

Second Row:

1st, 3rd People Handled Mugs	15.00 - 17.50 ea.
Bickering Mug (Possibly of Set)	18.00 - 20.00

Third Row:

All Mugs	15.00 - 17.50

Fourth Row:

Nude Lady Handled Mug	17.50 - 20.00
Parson Toby	50.00 - 65.00
Gentleman Toby	17.50 - 20.00

TOOTHPICK HOLDERS and BUD VASES

Among the more plentiful of "Occupied Japan" objects a few years ago, toothpick holders and bud vases are all but disappearing.

Few of these show any marked degree of workmanship; and on many, little paint was wasted. The top shelf is exempliary of the best to be expected in this category.

Top Row:

Cowboy and Dutch Girl	$ 12.00 - 15.00 ea.
Japanese Girl	12.00 - 15.00
Vase (Richly Painted, Gold Trim)	12.50 - 15.00

Second Row:

Vases	3.00 - 5.00
Dog and Birds	4.00 - 5.00
Man	5.00 - 6.00

Third Row:

Rabbits and Blue Vases	5.00 - 6.50 ea.
Scottie Dogs	5.00 - 7.50

Fourth Row:

Ox Cart	4.50 - 6.00
Pig	8.00 - 9.00
Accordian Player	3.50 - 4.00
Spotted Dog	5.00 - 6.00
Scottie	4.50 - 6.00

Fifth Row:

Vases	2.00 - 4.00
Animals	5.00 - 6.00

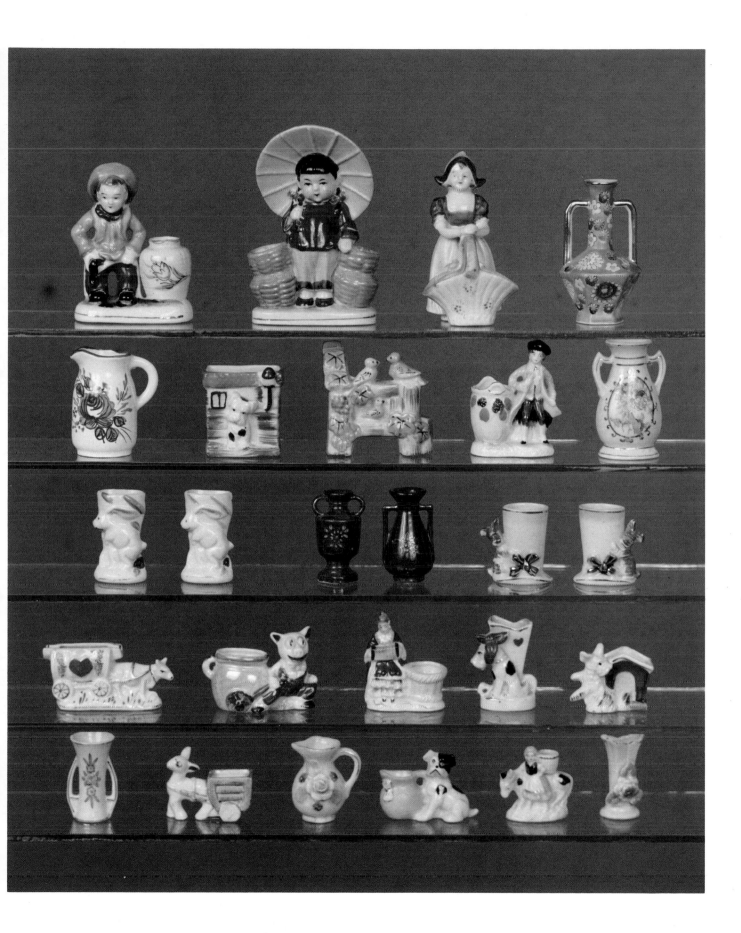

TOYS

I've had a time keeping my five and nine year old boys away from this department; so the toys of yesteryear still hold charm even if you do have to wind them instead of slapping in a battery.

The Studebaker and Chevrolets wind up and run; and the big red car is a "bumper" mobile. You wind it up and it goes forward until it bumps into something, then it will travel in reverse until it bumps something again, whereupon it will again go forward. "It's neat!" affirmed my son.

I've found two sets of checkers now but not a board marked "Occupied". There must surely still be one around.

The dagger, inflatable football and razzers are rubber toys: the football player, checkers and Yamato puzzle are all wood. The original box for the village is misplaced by the cars.

Top Row:	
Village (10 Pieces)	$ 25.00 - 30.00
Football Player	7.50 - 9.00
Second Row:	
Cars In Original Boxes	20.00 - 25.00
Wooden Puzzle	8.00 - 10.00
Rubber Knife	7.50 - 9.00
Third Row:	
Football	15.00 - 17.50
Checkers	10.00 - 12.50
Razzers	5.00 - 6.00

VASES

I assumed that after the seventy or so vases pictured in the first book, finding different ones might be rather difficult. However, there seem to be an unending variety of them!

On the second row you will see two similar vases, one with the flower in bud and one with that same flower in bloom.

In the third row, the bird on the middle vase is in relief.

The dragon head vase on the bottom shelf represents my best find. It's rice decoration and gold work are characteristic of the much earlier Nippon work. In fact, when I've had it at shows on display, numerous Nippon collectors have made a bee line for it and then examined it with a kind of sardonic impatience once they see it marked "Occupied".

Top Row:
1st, 6th and 7th Vases	$ 10.00 - 12.00 ea.
2nd, "Wedgewood" Vase	4.00 - 5.00
3rd, 4th and 5th Vases (3½-4")	6.00 - 7.50 ea.

Second Row:
1st and 6th Vase	5.00 - 7.50 ea.
2nd, 3rd, 4th Vases	15.00 - 17.50 ea.
5th Vase	17.50 - 20.00

Third Row:
1st and 5th, Pair	20.00 - 25.00
2nd, 3rd, 4th Vases	25.00 - 30.00 ea.

Fourth Row:
1st Vase	17.50 - 20.00
2nd Vase	20.00 - 22.50
Dragon Vase	50.00 - 60.00

PART II   FIGURINES

BISQUE FIGURINES

Bisque figurines appear to be the most highly prized of all the "Occupied Japan" figurines. Pictured are at lease two examples I feel to be the creme de la creme. While all of the cupid items have extremely fine coloring and detail, the easel and the hearts pieces are exceptional. I believe they are among the best examples of "Occupied Japan" bisque that I have ever seen.

Prices of the better Bisque figures are steadily increasing. However, I do not feel they have yet reached their peak due to the fact that the collecting of "Occupied Japan" objects is just coming of age. As more and more collectors enter the field and become aware of the "quality" merchandise, demand should be increased. Therefore, today's bargain could be tomorrow's steal.

Once an "Occupied" figurine reaches a height of eight inches or beyond, its value vastly increases due to scarcity. You can find any number of figurines in the four to seven and a half inch variety; thus, the taller the figurine, the better its value becomes.

The male and female figurines coupled in the photograph are not a pair. We "married" this 15½" tall male to the 14½" tall female to show you that you don't necessarily have to find pairs of statuettes to display them to advantage. On close examination, you will notice that the bases don't match and that the female is a trifle more colorful than the male; but before I pointed out the differences, I'll bet you had accepted them as a pair. The point of this exercise is to keep you from passing by a taller "Occupied Japan" figurine because it's mate is absent. There is always the chance of finding the exact mate; there is every chance of pairing the figure successfully with another of similar coloring; if nothing else, you can use the taller figure in trade for something you want; whatever you do, don't leave a taller figurine behind. You'll live to rue the day!

Top Row:	
Man, 15½"	$ 65.00 - 75.00
Lady, 14½"	50.00 - 60.00
Second Row:	
Cupid and Swan	27.50 - 30.00
Cupid Artist	45.00 - 50.00
Cupid Standing	25.00 - 30.00
Third Row:	
"Hummel-like" boy and girl	20.00 - 25.00 ea.
Cupid and Heart	45.00 - 50.00
Seated Musician	20.00 - 25.00

BISQUE FIGURINES (Con't.)

Top Row:
Bust of Man	$ 22.50 - 25.00
Lady Vase	22.50 - 25.00

Second Row:
Caped Boy and Girl	20.00 - 22.50 ea.
Mexican with Donkey (Approx. 8")	20.00 - 22.50
Lady with Basket	17.50 - 20.00

Third Row:
Colonial Man	12.00 - 15.00
Japanese Samurai	17.50 - 20.00
Peasant Girl Planter	30.00 - 35.00

CHILDREN

There are some collectors who collect any type of child figurine, from the lesser quality all the way to the "Hummel" type. On the second row are three "Hummel" types which are repeated on the next page.

Notice the pained expression on the child in the last row, the one with the bee on his bottom!

Top Row:
1st, 2nd, 4th and 5th Children	$ 6.50 - 7.50
3rd Boy and Boy with Pig	10.00 - 12.50

Second Row:
Girl on Fence	12.50 - 15.00
Girl in Cape	12.50 - 15.00
Girl with Geese	20.00 - 25.00
Girls with Baskets	20.00 - 25.00 ea.

Third Row:
Musicians	10.00 - 12.00

Fourth Row:
Girl with Doll	8.00 - 10.00
Girl with Accordian	8.50 - 10.00
Baby with Bee	12.50 - 15.00
Double Figure with Umbrella	10.00 - 12.50
Tiny Girl in Green	3.50 - 4.50

CHILDREN - "HUMMEL TYPE"

The imitation of Hummel works is very evident on the following page. If you can't afford the genuine 1950 Hummels, then look to the "Occupied Japan" imitations which are cute, affordable and collectible. Hummel-like "Occupied Japan" figurines are perhaps the most underpriced of all at present.

The "Hummel-like" figurines shown are among the best examples to be found. Many can be found which are very crude, poorly painted, poorly molded, etc. These lesser types may have some extra value as "Hummel-like" but not a great deal.

Remember, figurines with two or more figures are better than single figured ones.

Top Row:
Boy and Girl (Approx. 8 inches) $ 20.00 - 25.00 ea.;
60.00 pr.

Second Row:
Girl and Doll	30.00 - 35.00
Children with Boat	30.00 - 35.00
Children with Umbrella	30.00 - 35.00

Third Row:
Walking Boy (Larger of Two)	20.00 - 25.00
Artist and Palette	30.00 - 35.00
Umbrella Boy	20.00 - 25.00
Walking Boy (Smaller of Two)	12.50 - 15.00
Hiker	12.50 - 15.00

Fourth Row:
Girls with Geese	20.00 - 25.00
Girl Feeding Geese	15.00 - 17.50
Girls with Baskets	20.00 - 25.00 ea.

DELFT BLUE FIGURINES

Prices observed on delft figurines at antique shows and flea markets have frankly astounded me. I knew there were collectors of the delft blue; but I hadn't known there were enough to zoom prices so far above ordinary statues.

I have found that some delft collectors are so purist as to not allow any color but blue and white to be shown; others seem to like the bits of color noticeable on a couple of the ladies shown here.

Top Row:
Lady and Gentleman, Paired $ 25.00 - 30.00 ea.

Second Row:
Dutch Children	15.00 - 20.00 ea.
Lady Holding Hat	17.50 - 20.00
Dancing Lady	17.50 - 20.00

Third Row:
Tambourine Player	20.00 - 25.00
Dancer	25.00 - 30.00
Tiered Skirted Lady	25.00 - 30.00

ELVES AND PIXIES

Elves and pixies number among the most adorable of the O.J. collectibles. Unfortunately for collectors, their appeal to John Q. Public as well as avid "Occupied" fans causes the price to rise because the demand for these items is greater than for others.

In case you're a little fuzzy on your elves and pixies; the pixies have ruffled hats and the elves have cone shaped ones.

Generally speaking, elves with varying colored suits astride insects or animals show more detail and workmanship than do elves with suits of a single color; hence the price discrepancy between the elves riding insects on the last row and their more colorful kinsmen above.

Top Row:
Green Pixies $ 12.50 - 15.00 ea.
Planter Pixie   15.00 - 17.50

Second Row:
Elves Riding Insects/Animals   22.50 - 25.00

Third Row:
Mushroom Elves   10.00 - 12.00
Elf Astride Insect   22.50 - 25.00

Fourth Row:
Pink Suited Elves   15.00 - 17.50

FIGURINE GROUPS

By far the most difficult pieces of "Occupied Japan" to acquire are the figurines with two or more figures on one base. When found, they usually depict a couple.

The top row shows like statutes in reversed positions, but painted differently. Originally, you could buy these figurines in pairs or one for each end of the mantel so to speak. I have the mates to both of these, but I wanted to show you that like figurines were painted in a multitude of ways to blend with different decors.

I have seen the Cinderella coach put on a metal base and made into a lamp.

The little Dutch Boy and Girl in the clinch is a holder for toothbrushes.

Top Row:

First and Third Couple	$ 25.00 - 30.00 ea.
Coach	45.00 - 50.00

Second Row:

Couple with Bench, Artist Signed	25.00 - 30.00
Standing Couple	27.50 - 30.00
Seated Couple	17.50 - 20.00
Seated Couple, Small, Artist Signed	20.00 - 25.00

Third Row:

1st and 3rd Courting Couple	22.50 - 25.00
Seated Red Haired Couple	12.50 - 15.00

Bottom Row:

Oriental Couple	20.00 - 22.50
Dutch Children Toothbrush Holder	20.00 - 25.00

ORIENTAL FIGURINES

As in most categories, there are a multitude of inferiorly made statues of Orientals. However, for the most part, the quality of the ones shown is superior. The painting is colorful and detailed and representative of the culture from which it originated. (You will have noticed that the Japanese statues of Americans tend to be of Colonial America.)

Top Row:

Girl, 12″ Tall	$ 22.50 - 25.00
2nd and 5th Dancers	20.00 - 22.50
3rd and 4th	17.50 - 20.00 ea.

Second Row:

1st and 6th Small Figures	8.50 - 10.00
2nd and 5th Men, Nice Detail	20.00 - 25.00 ea.
3rd Girl with Fan	10.00 - 12.50
4th Male Musician	10.00 - 12.00

Third Row:

1st and 5th Small Figures	6.00 - 7.00 ea.
2nd Performer, Mate to Above	8.50 - 10.00
Reclining Man	10.00 - 12.50
Couple	8.50 - 10.00

ORIENTAL PAIRS

Again, detail and color of the pairs shown make them of exceptional quality. I tended to ignore couples I found without good coloring.

These statues are **priced as pairs**. Usually, you can buy a single for less than half of the total price charged for a pair. At least, this has been my experience. However, when you purchase a single figurine and search five or six years for a mate, you can understand why paired items must command a higher price.

Top Row:

Oriental Pair	$ 50.00 - 55.00
Trousered Oriental Pair	45.00 - 50.00

Second Row:

First Pair Orientals	35.00 - 40.00
Black Based Orientals	30.00 - 35.00

Third Row:

Coolie Hatted Pair	22.50 - 25.00
Animated Pair Orientals	25.00 - 30.00

Fourth Row:

Flared Trousered Pair	30.00 - 35.00
Second Pair	30.00 - 35.00

PAIRS of FIGURINES

As stated previously, there is a small premium paid for pairs of figurines due to their still being together and undamaged after a thirty year time lapse. You might think of it as time and gasoline or postage saved in the long run. Size and richness of design and painting are things to consider when purchasing pairs of figurines. Figurines of more than eight inches in height are desirable; figurines of fourteen inches tall, or better, are extremely desirable and practically impossible to find.

The thing I find impossible to understand is that people will go to the department store and pay $25 to $50 for a pair of **new** figurines to grace their living room decor. There are probably millions of pairs just like them. They could have bought a pair of collectible figurines for about the same money at the local antique store: Why buy "nothing" when you could have "something" for the same money?

Please notice the couple on page 99 with their animals.

Top Row:
Colonial Couple $100.00 -125.00 pr.

Second Row:
Couple in Blue and Pink,
   12″   75.00 - 85.00

Third Row:
Hatted Pair, Approx. 12″   60.00 - 75.00
Courting Couple, Approx.
   12″   60.00 - 75.00

Bottom Row:
Musicians Couple,
   Approx. 10″   50.00 - 60.00
Seated Pair, 6″   30.00 - 35.00

(See Page 98)
Top Row:
Hatted Colonials, Approx.
   12″ $ 50.00 - 60.00 pr.
Red Haired Colonials,
   11½″   35.00 - 40.00 pr.

Second Row:
First and Third Pair,
   Approx. 10″   35.00 - 40.00
Second Pair Colonials,
   11½″   37.50 - 42.50 pr

Third Row:
First and Fourth Pairs,
   Approx. 6″   17.50 - 20.00 pr
Musical Pair   32.50 - 35.00
Pair in Blue Tones   17.50 - 20.00

(See Page 99)
Top Row:
Musical Couples $ 25.00 - 30.00

Second Row:
First Pair (Bisque),
   Approx. 10″   50.00 - 60.00
Second Pair   20.00 - 25.00
Pair Dancers (Bisque),
   10″   35.00 - 40.00

Third Row:
1st and 3rd Pair, Seated   35.00 - 40.00
2nd Pair, Orientals, Bis-
   que, Approx. 9″   40.00 - 45.00

SHELF SITTERS and INCENSE BURNERS

Shelf sitters are possibly the most unique items to be found among figurines in "Occupied Japan". Fishermen types are common themes of this type figurine though they're often found today minus their fishing poles as is the case with the Oriental fisherman on the end of the second row. His friend at the opposite end who's measuring with his hands must be discussing the one that got away.

You can see two different sizes of "Little Boy Blue" recliners.

The top row features incense burners. These were very popular with the "hippies" a few years ago. People tend to spray fragrances into the homes today; but occasionally it might be nice to scent it in a more old fashioned manner.

Top Row:
Incense Burners	$ 15.00 - 17.50

Second Row:
Orientals (At End of Row)	20.00 - 22.50 ea.
Mandolin and Flute Players	10.00 - 12.00 ea.
3rd and 4th Figures	12.50 - 15.00

Third Row:
1st Pair	10.00 - 12.00 ea.
3rd Double Figure, Boy & Girl	10.00 - 12.00
Girl in Lavender (Probably One of Pair)	12.50 - 15.00
Colonial Man (Probably One of Pair)	12.00 - 15.00

Fourth Row:
Reclining Oriental	9.00 - 11.00
Smaller Boy Blue	9.00 - 10.00
Larger Boy Blue	13.50 - 15.00
Seated Tyrolienne Boy	10.00 - 12.00

STATUETTES

There are a multitude of single statuettes on the next three pages covering a range of quality and ideas.

Notice that the Oriental figure, top row center, is the same one used for the lamp in said section.

Second row center is an example of netting or crinoline figures that was popular during the 1950's. You usually find this on the ballet figurines; I was interested in getting this full skirted figure with netting.

The bride and groom figures on page 105 are hard to find marked. I found the set on the left in a box of twelve. The box was marked "Occupied" but the figures themselves were just marked "Japan".

On the third row is a Negro shoe shine boy, a blatant stereotype that one wouldn't find marketed today. One Negro lady said they used to buy these out of their local dime store and take them home and break them up. Maybe that explains why the Negro "Occupied Japan" work is in such short supply today?

Top Row:

1st and 5th	$ 15.00 - 17.50
2nd and 4th	22.00 - 25.00
3rd (Seen as Lamp Base)	22.50 - 25.00

Second Row:

1st Colonial	20.00 - 25.00
Lady with Dog	20.00 - 25.00
Lady with Net Dress	35.00 - 40.00
Gaucho with Guitar	15.00 - 17.50
Lady in Pink and White	10.00 - 12.00

Third Row:

Colonial in Tri-Cornered Hat, 11″	20.00 - 22.50
Lady with Horn, Approx. 11″	20.00 - 22.50
Lady with Accordian, Approx. 10″	17.50 - 20.00

(See Page 104)

Top Row:

1st, 2nd, 4th Lady	5.00 - 6.50
Dutch Girl with Buckets	17.50 - 20.00

Second Row:

1st and 4th Colonials	10.00 - 12.50
2nd and 3rd	13.00 - 15.00
5th Lady	8.00 - 10.00

Third Row:

1st and 5th Musicians	12.50 - 15.00
2nd and 4th Ladies	10.00 - 12.50
Lady with Flower Basket	12.00 - 15.00

Fourth Row:

1st, 2nd, 3rd Colonials	12.50 - 15.00
4th Lady	17.50 - 20.00
Lady with Dog	20.00 - 22.50

(See Page 105)

Top Row:

Bride and Groom, 4¼″	20.00 - 25.00
Bride and Groom, 5″	25.00 - 30.00
Bride and Groom, 3½″	15.00 - 17.50

Second Row:

Wood-Like Dwarves, 1st and 6th	8.00 - 10.00
Wood-Like Dwarves, 2nd thru 5th	10.00 - 12.00

Third Row:

1st and 2nd Ladies	3.00 - 5.00
Negro Match Holder	17.00 - 20.00
Shoe Shine Boy	30.00 - 35.00
African Boy	15.00 - 20.00
Uncle Sam, 5″	20.00 - 25.00

Fourth Row:

Indian Salt Shakers (Each End)	10.00 - 12.00 pr.
3rd and 6th Indian	8.00 - 10.00 ea.
4th Chief	17.00 - 20.00
5th Chief	20.00 - 25.00

Fifth Row:

Ballerina with Net Skirt	15.00 - 17.50
2nd, 3rd, 6th Ladies	10.00 - 12.50
4th Lady in Yellow Skirt, Bisque	17.50 - 20.00
5th Dancer	8.00 - 10.00

UNUSUAL "OCCUPIED JAPAN" OBJECTS

This 24″ celluloid stork came out of a baby shop display in the Pittsburg area. It's the largest celluloid item I've ever come across.

The mother of pearl inlay lamp measures 24″ just to the light socket. The entire lamp measures in excess of three feet including the finial on top. I hope the pagoda scene will show as well in print as is does on the negative I'm viewing as I write.

This lamp is one of a pair which I found in California. They came with shades which we removed so as to better show you the detail of the inlay scene.

Lamp	$100.00 - 125.00
Stork	50.00 - 65.00

LATE ARRIVALS

It never fails! You carefully gather materials for a couple of years; you spend a week unwrapping and grouping things for the intense three days of photographing from daylight to dark; you photograph, get everything repacked and get the proofs back; then, for the next three weeks "Occupied Japan" will literally fall on you from everywhere — people stopping want to sell some, a nearby show has a whole display of it, someone calls about the biggest, most fantastic piece you ever heard of! Why can it never happen BEFORE the photography session?

This year, when so much "good stuff" showed up afterward, I just gathered it all together and had the photographer make more pictures regardless of categories; I couldn't have you miss the gigantic 15½ inch pair of figurines in bisque, the five little "Hummel" type children, or the mate to the planter of the girl with her tongue out, etc.

Hodge-podge though it is, I hope you'll think it worth including.

Bisque Colonial Pair, 15½"	$150.00 - 175.00
Bisque Cavalier, 14"	60.00 - 65.00

(See Page 110)

Top Row:

Satsuma-like Tea Pot (Other Pieces Likely)	$ 35.00 - 40.00
"Hummel-like" Soldier Children	30.00 - 35.00
"Hummel-like" Children with Boat	30.00 - 35.00

Second Row:

Children Planters, Pair	35.00 - 45.00
Negro Shelf Sitter	15.00 - 20.00
Horned Bugle Boy Devil in Bisque	20.00 - 22.50
Cupid and Shell Planters, Pair	30.00 - 35.00

Third Row:

Celluloid Cowboy with Wind Up Bucking Horse	30.00 - 35.00
"Hummel-like" Children with Dogs	30.00 - 35.00 ea.

(See Page 111)

Top Row:

Cow Creamer	$ 25.00 - 30.00

Second Row:

Bird Shaker and Mustard Set	22.50 - 25.00
Old Oriental	12.50 - 15.00
Sassy Boy Planter (Mate Shown Elsewhere)	12.50 - 15.00

Third Row:

Strawberry Shakers in Basket	12.00 - 15.00
Pink Cigarette Box (Trays Within)	15.00 - 20.00
Black and White Cup and Saucer	10.00 - 12.50
Deer	4.00 - 6.00

Fourth Row:

Demitasse Cup and Saucer	10.00 - 12.00 ea
Ash Tray to Cigarette Box (Alone)	3.00 - 3.50 ea
Coffee Pot Shakers	10.00 - 12.00 pr
Pixie Toothpick Holder	10.00 - 12.00

Fifth Row:

Odd Tea Kettle Shakers	3.00 - 3.50 ea

(See Page 112)

Top Row:

Match Safe Wall Hanger	$ 30.00 - 35.00
Grampa with Bug	10.00 - 12.00
Dutch Girl Marmalade	12.00 - 15.00

Second Row:

Lighted (Electric) Wall Plaque, Bisque	30.00 - 35.00
Large Duck Plaque	12.50 - 15.00
Mexican Toothpick Holder	6.00 - 7.00

Third Row:

Fruit Plate for Hanging (Shown Upside Down)	8.00 - 10.00

Smaller Duck Plaque	8.00 - 10.00
Cup and Saucer	12.50 - 15.00

Fourth Row:

Donkey Cart Planter	3.50 - 4.50
Decorative Tray	2.50 - 3.50
Strawberry Covered Jar	10.00 - 12.00
Cobalt Blue Powder Jar, Hinged	40.00 - 50.00

Fifth Row:

Dog Relish (Head Lifts for Further Serving Capacity)	30.00 - 35.00
Cow Creamer	25.00 - 30.00